Spanish Verb
Practice Workbook

Susan Stubbs

ISBN: 9798488744684

Introduction to
Spanish Verb Practice Workbook

Getting the verbs straightened out was always the toughest part for me as a native English speaker trying to learn Spanish. I created this workbook because it is what I have needed at every level in my Spanish language studies.

The workbook has a very simple but effective design for you to use at whatever level you are working on.

Choose the verb. Choose the tense. Look up the conjugations for that verb in that tense and fill in the table. Find or create phrases or sentences using your verb and tense. Write them as examples on the lines provided.

Read them aloud to practice your pronunciation and to help them stick in your mind.

I recommend writing by hand. This is more effective than just reading or even typing on the computer. The physical act of writing has been shown to improve mental processing and assimilation of information. It focuses your mind on constructing sentences and their meanings. When you say them aloud, it helps you use your other senses. The more senses you use, the more you will recall.

If you want to make a note of what or why something is happening in the grammar of the sentence - do it. If you need to remember the meaning of a phrase, noun, or adjective - write it. This is your notebook to use as you see fit.

You are in charge of your own learning. The best examples are those that you expect to need for conversation. The best way to remember the language is to use it daily in practical ways.

When you learn languages, any content can become a source of learning. Collect your sentences from the topics that really interest you whether they are entertainment, social media, shows, sports, or the news. Choose the verbs from phrases you find in your textbooks, reading, or hear in songs, or Spanish conversation.

Choose your verb tenses either by what you are finding difficult to master, or that you need to use to make a request, ask a question, or tell a story. Your sentences can be serious or silly. The more vivid your examples are, the more memorable they will be.

Don't just write in this workbook and expect that is all you need to do. Integrate the language into your daily life. Use the verbs and the tenses you are studying as often as possible..

The following is an example of how I would use the worksheets to examine the verb IR (to go) and its reflexive companion verb IRSE (to leave) in the present tense. I have filled in only part of this sheet, so if you wish, think of a few more sentences using IR or IRSE in the present tense. Can you make them more memorable than mine?

You probably already know each of the words on the worksheet, but just in case you don't, here are their working definitions and a glossary of the 14 (or 15 counting the imperative) Spanish verb tenses.

Best Regards

Susan Stubbs

I plan to publish more of my personal exercises booklets.
If you are interested in getting them or have any Questions? Email me at InfoLlama @mail.com

Glossary

Infinitivo	Infinitive (-ar, -er -ir form of the verb)
¿Reflejo?	Reflex? (does one do the action to oneself)
Sí, No	Yes, No
Significado	Meaning
Tiempo verbal	Verb tense
¿Irregular?	Irregular? (does the root stay the same or change in some conjugations?)
Yo	I
Nosotros	We
Tú	You
Vosotros	You
Él, ,	He, ,
Ella,	She,
Usted	You
Ellos	They
Ellas,	They,
Ustedes	You
Frases	Phrases

Me voy de la escuela a las cuatro. (Irse)

Mañana vamos al campo. (Ir)

¿Ustedes van al cine todos los fines de semana? (Ir)

¿Tú te vas temprano? (Irse)

I leave school at four o'clock.

Tomorrow we go to the countryside.

Do you go to the movies every weekend?

Do you leave early?

Here are some terms used to describe tenses of verbs listed by Christopher; Theodore Kendris. in 501 Spanish Verbs published by Barrons Educational Series:

Gerundio	Gerund
Pasado participio	Past participle
1 presente de indicativo	1 present indicative
2 imperfecto de indicativo	2 imperfect of indicative
3 pretérito	3 preterite
4 futuro	4 future
5 potencial simple (condicional)	5 simple potential (conditional)
6 presente de subjuntivo	6 present subjunctive
7 imperfecto de subjuntivo	7 imperfect subjunctive
Imperativo	Imperative
8 perfecto de indicativo	8 perfect of indicative
9 pluscuamperfecto de indicativo	9 pluperfect of indicative
10 pretérito anterior	10 preterite past tense
11 futuro perfecto	11 future perfect
12 potencial compuesto	12 compound potential
13 perfecto de subjuntivo	13 perfect subjunctive
14 pluscuamperfecto de subjuntivo	14 pluperfect subjunctive past perfect

Infinitivo *Ir, Irse*   ¿Reflejo?   Sí   No

Significado *to go, to leave*

Pasado participio   Gerundio
(—ado)   *ido*   (—ando)   *yendo, yéndose*

Tiempo verbal   *presente*   ¿Irregular?   Sí   No

Yo	*voy, me voy*	Nosotros	*vamos, nos vamos*
Tú	*vas, te va*	Vosotros	*Vosotros vais, Os vais*
Él, Ella, Usted	*va, se va*	Ellos, Ellas, Ustedes	*van, se van*

Frases: *Mañana vamos al campo. (Ir)*

¿Ustedes van al cine todos los fines de semana? (Ir)

Me voy de la escuela a las cuatro. (Irse)

¿Tú te vas temprano? (Irse)

NOTES: IR can be used present tense "IR a" + infinitive

to indicate future: "Voy a estudiar." (I am going to study.)

and in imperfect indicative (past progressive tense) to indicate

a past action: "Yo iba a estudiar." (I was going to study.) ETC.

Infinitivo _____ ¿Reflejo? Sí No

Significado _____

Pasado participio _____ Gerundio _____
(—ado)   (—ando)

Tiempo verbal _____   ¿Irregular? Sí No

Yo _____   Nosotros _____

Tú _____   Vosotros _____

Él, Ella,   Ellos, Ellas,
Usted _____   Ustedes _____

Frases:
_____
_____
_____
_____
_____
_____
_____
_____
_____
_____
_____

Infinitivo _____ ¿Reflejo?   Sí   No

Significado _____

Pasado participio   Gerundio
(—ado) _____   (—ando) _____

Tiempo verbal _____   ¿Irregular?   Sí   No

Yo _____   Nosotros _____

Tú _____   Vosotros _____

Él, Ella,   Ellos, Ellas,
Usted _____   Ustedes _____

Frases: _____

_____

_____

_____

_____

_____

_____

_____

_____

_____

_____

_____

_____

Infinitivo _____ ¿Reflejo?   Sí   No

Significado _____

Pasado participio   Gerundio
(—ado) _____   (—ando) _____

Tiempo verbal _____ ¿Irregular?   Sí   No

Yo _____   Nosotros _____

Tú _____   Vosotros _____

Él, Ella,   Ellos, Ellas,
Usted _____   Ustedes _____

Frases: _____

_____

_____

_____

_____

_____

_____

_____

_____

_____

_____

_____

_____

Infinitivo _____   ¿Reflejo?   Sí   No

Significado _____

Pasado participio _____   Gerundio _____
(—ado)   (—ando)

Tiempo verbal _____   ¿Irregular?   Sí   No

Yo _____   Nosotros _____

Tú _____   Vosotros _____

Él, Ella, _____   Ellos, Ellas, _____
Usted   Ustedes

Frases: _____

_____

_____

_____

_____

_____

_____

_____

_____

_____

_____

_____

Infinitivo _____   ¿Reflejo?   Sí   No

Significado _____

Infinitivo _____   ¿Reflejo?   Sí   No

Significado _____

Pasado participio   Gerundio
(—ado) _____   (—ando) _____

Tiempo verbal _____   ¿Irregular?   Sí   No

Yo _____   Nosotros _____

Tú _____   Vosotros _____

Él, Ella,   Ellos, Ellas,
Usted _____   Ustedes _____

Frases:
_____
_____
_____
_____
_____
_____
_____
_____
_____
_____
_____
_____

Infinitivo _____   ¿Reflejo?   Sí   No

Significado _____

Pasado participio _____   Gerundio _____
(—ado)   (—ando)

Tiempo verbal _____   ¿Irregular?   Sí   No

Yo _____   Nosotros _____

Tú _____   Vosotros _____

Él, Ella,   Ellos, Ellas,
Usted _____   Ustedes _____

Frases: _____

_____

_____

_____

_____

_____

_____

_____

_____

_____

_____

_____

_____

Infinitivo _____ ¿Reflejo?   Sí   No

Significado _____

Pasado participio   Gerundio
(—ado) _____   (—ando) _____

Tiempo verbal _____ ¿Irregular?   Sí   No

Yo _____   Nosotros _____

Tú _____   Vosotros _____

Él, Ella,   Ellos, Ellas,
Usted _____   Ustedes _____

Frases: _____

_____

_____

_____

_____

_____

_____

_____

_____

_____

_____

_____

Infinitivo _____ ¿Reflejo?   Sí   No

Significado _____

Pasado participio   Gerundio
(—ado) _____   (—ando) _____

Tiempo verbal _____ ¿Irregular?   Sí   No

Yo _____   Nosotros _____

Tú _____   Vosotros _____

Él, Ella,   Ellos, Ellas,
Usted _____   Ustedes _____

Frases:
_____

_____

_____

_____

_____

_____

_____

_____

_____

_____

_____

_____

Infinitivo _____ ¿Reflejo?   Sí   No

Significado _____

Pasado participio   Gerundio
(—ado) _____   (—ando) _____

Tiempo verbal _____   ¿Irregular?   Sí   No

Yo _____   Nosotros _____

Tú _____   Vosotros _____

Él, Ella,   Ellos, Ellas,
Usted _____   Ustedes _____

Frases: _____

_____

_____

_____

_____

_____

_____

_____

_____

_____

_____

_____

Infinitivo _____ ¿Reflejo?   Sí   No

Significado _____

Pasado participio   Gerundio
(—ado) _____   (—ando) _____

Tiempo verbal _____ ¿Irregular?   Sí   No

Yo _____   Nosotros _____

Tú _____   Vosotros _____

Él, Ella,   Ellos, Ellas,
Usted _____   Ustedes _____

Frases:
_____
_____
_____
_____
_____
_____
_____
_____
_____
_____
_____
_____
_____

Infinitivo _____   ¿Reflejo?   Sí   No

Significado _____

Pasado participio   Gerundio
(—ado) _____   (—ando) _____

Tiempo verbal _____   ¿Irregular?   Sí   No

Yo _____   Nosotros _____

Tú _____   Vosotros _____

Él, Ella,   Ellos, Ellas,
Usted _____   Ustedes _____

Frases: _____

_____

_____

_____

_____

_____

_____

_____

_____

_____

_____

_____

Infinitivo _____   ¿Reflejo?   Sí   No

Significado _____

Pasado participio   Gerundio
(—ado) _____   (—ando) _____

Tiempo verbal _____   ¿Irregular?   Sí   No

Yo _____   Nosotros _____

Tú _____   Vosotros _____

Él, Ella,   Ellos, Ellas,
Usted _____   Ustedes _____

Frases: _____

_____

_____

_____

_____

_____

_____

_____

_____

_____

_____

_____

_____

Infinitivo _____   ¿Reflejo?   Sí   No

Significado _____

Pasado participio   Gerundio
(—ado) _____   (—ando) _____

Tiempo verbal _____   ¿Irregular?   Sí   No

Yo _____   Nosotros _____

Tú _____   Vosotros _____

Él, Ella,   Ellos, Ellas,
Usted _____   Ustedes _____

Frases:

_____

_____

_____

_____

_____

_____

_____

_____

_____

_____

_____

Infinitivo .... ¿Reflejo?   Sí   No

Significado ....

Pasado participio   Gerundio
(—ado) .... (—ando) ....

Tiempo verbal .... ¿Irregular?   Sí   No

Yo .... Nosotros ....

Tú .... Vosotros ....

Él, Ella,   Ellos, Ellas,
Usted .... Ustedes ....

Frases: ....

....

....

....

....

....

....

....

....

....

....

....

....

Infinitivo _____ ¿Reflejo?   Sí   No

Significado _____

Pasado participio   Gerundio
(—ado) _____   (—ando) _____

Tiempo verbal _____   ¿Irregular?   Sí   No

Yo _____   Nosotros _____

Tú _____   Vosotros _____

Él, Ella,   Ellos, Ellas,
Usted _____   Ustedes _____

Frases: _____

_____

_____

_____

_____

_____

_____

_____

_____

_____

_____

_____

Infinitivo _____ ¿Reflejo?   Sí   No

Significado _____

Pasado participio   Gerundio
(—ado) _____   (—ando) _____

Tiempo verbal _____   ¿Irregular?   Sí   No

Yo _____   Nosotros _____

Tú _____   Vosotros _____

Él, Ella,   Ellos, Ellas,
Usted _____   Ustedes _____

Frases:

_____

_____

_____

_____

_____

_____

_____

_____

_____

_____

_____

Infinitivo _____ ¿Reflejo?   Sí   No

Significado _____

Pasado participio   Gerundio
(—ado)   (—ando)
_____   _____

Tiempo verbal _____ ¿Irregular?   Sí   No

Yo _____   Nosotros _____

Tú _____   Vosotros _____

Él, Ella,   Ellos, Ellas,
Usted _____   Ustedes _____

Frases: _____

_____

_____

_____

_____

_____

_____

_____

_____

_____

_____

_____

_____

Infinitivo _____ ¿Reflejo?   Sí   No

Significado _____

Pasado participio   Gerundio
(—ado) _____   (—ando) _____

Tiempo verbal _____ ¿Irregular?   Sí   No

Yo _____   Nosotros _____

Tú _____   Vosotros _____

Él, Ella,   Ellos, Ellas,
Usted _____   Ustedes _____

Frases: _____

_____

_____

_____

_____

_____

_____

_____

_____

_____

_____

_____

Infinitivo _____ ¿Reflejo?   Sí   No

Significado _____

Pasado participio   Gerundio
(—ado)   (—ando)
_____   _____

Tiempo verbal _____ ¿Irregular?   Sí   No

Yo _____   Nosotros _____

Tú _____   Vosotros _____

Él, Ella,   Ellos, Ellas,
Usted _____ Ustedes _____

Frases: _____

_____

_____

_____

_____

_____

_____

_____

_____

_____

_____

_____

_____

_____

Infinitivo _____ ¿Reflejo?   Sí   No

Significado _____

Pasado participio _____   Gerundio _____
(—ado)   (—ando)

Tiempo verbal _____   ¿Irregular?   Sí   No

Yo _____   Nosotros _____

Tú _____   Vosotros _____

Él, Ella,   Ellos, Ellas,
Usted _____   Ustedes _____

Frases: _____

_____

_____

_____

_____

_____

_____

_____

_____

_____

_____

_____

Infinitivo _____   ¿Reflejo?   Sí   No

Significado _____

Pasado participio   Gerundio
(—ado) _____   (—ando) _____

Tiempo verbal _____   ¿Irregular?   Sí   No

Yo _____   Nosotros _____

Tú _____   Vosotros _____

Él, Ella,   Ellos, Ellas,
Usted _____   Ustedes _____

Frases: _____

_____

_____

_____

_____

_____

_____

_____

_____

_____

_____

_____

_____

_____

Infinitivo _____ ¿Reflejo?   Sí   No

Significado _____

Pasado participio   Gerundio
(—ado)   _____   (—ando)   _____

Tiempo verbal _____ ¿Irregular?   Sí   No

Yo   _____   Nosotros _____

Tú   _____   Vosotros _____

Él, Ella,   Ellos, Ellas,
Usted   _____   Ustedes   _____

Frases: _____

_____

_____

_____

_____

_____

_____

_____

_____

_____

_____

Infinitivo _____   ¿Reflejo?   Sí   No

Significado _____

Pasado participio   Gerundio
(—ado) _____   (—ando) _____

Tiempo verbal _____   ¿Irregular?   Sí   No

Yo _____   Nosotros _____

Tú _____   Vosotros _____

Él, Ella,   Ellos, Ellas,
Usted _____   Ustedes _____

Frases:

_____

_____

_____

_____

_____

_____

_____

_____

_____

_____

_____

_____

Infinitivo _____ ¿Reflejo?   Sí   No

Significado _____

Pasado participio   Gerundio
(—ado) _____   (—ando) _____

Tiempo verbal _____ ¿Irregular?   Sí   No

Yo _____   Nosotros _____

Tú _____   Vosotros _____

Él, Ella,   Ellos, Ellas,
Usted _____ Ustedes _____

Frases:

_____

_____

_____

_____

_____

_____

_____

_____

_____

_____

_____

Infinitivo _____ ¿Reflejo? Sí No

Significado _____

Pasado participio   Gerundio
(—ado) _____ (—ando) _____

Tiempo verbal _____ ¿Irregular? Sí No

Yo _____ Nosotros _____

Tú _____ Vosotros _____

Él, Ella,   Ellos, Ellas,
Usted _____ Ustedes _____

Frases: _____

_____

_____

_____

_____

_____

_____

_____

_____

_____

_____

_____

Infinitivo _____ ¿Reflejo? Sí No

Infinitivo _____ ¿Reflejo?   Sí   No

Significado _____

Pasado participio   Gerundio
(—ado) _____   (—ando) _____

Tiempo verbal _____   ¿Irregular?   Sí   No

Yo _____   Nosotros _____

Tú _____   Vosotros _____

Él, Ella,   Ellos, Ellas,
Usted _____   Ustedes _____

Frases: _____

_____

_____

_____

_____

_____

_____

_____

_____

_____

_____

Infinitivo _____ ¿Reflejo?   Sí   No

Significado _____

Pasado participio   Gerundio
(—ado) _____   (—ando) _____

Tiempo verbal _____   ¿Irregular?   Sí   No

Yo _____   Nosotros _____

Tú _____   Vosotros _____

Él, Ella,   Ellos, Ellas,
Usted _____   Ustedes _____

Frases: _____

Infinitivo _____ ¿Reflejo?   Sí   No

Significado _____

Pasado participio   Gerundio
(—ado) _____   (—ando) _____

Tiempo verbal _____   ¿Irregular?   Sí   No

Yo _____   Nosotros _____

Tú _____   Vosotros _____

Él, Ella,   Ellos, Ellas,
Usted _____   Ustedes _____

Frases:

_____

_____

_____

_____

_____

_____

_____

_____

_____

_____

_____

Infinitivo _____ ¿Reflejo?   Sí   No

Infinitivo _____ ¿Reflejo?   Sí   No

Significado _____

Pasado participio _____ Gerundio _____
(—ado)   (—ando)

Tiempo verbal _____ ¿Irregular?   Sí   No

Yo _____   Nosotros _____

Tú _____   Vosotros _____

Él, Ella, _____ Ellos, Ellas, _____
Usted   Ustedes

Frases:

_____

_____

_____

_____

_____

_____

_____

_____

_____

_____

_____

_____

Infinitivo _____ ¿Reflejo?   Sí   No

Significado _____

Pasado participio   Gerundio
(—ado) _____   (—ando) _____

Tiempo verbal _____   ¿Irregular?   Sí   No

Yo _____   Nosotros _____

Tú _____   Vosotros _____

Él, Ella,   Ellos, Ellas,
Usted _____   Ustedes _____

Frases: _____

_____

_____

_____

_____

_____

_____

_____

_____

_____

_____

_____

Infinitivo _____   ¿Reflejo?   Sí   No

Significado _____

Pasado participio   Gerundio
(—ado)   (—ando)
_____   _____

Tiempo verbal _____   ¿Irregular?   Sí   No

Yo _____   Nosotros _____

Tú _____   Vosotros _____

Él, Ella,   Ellos, Ellas,
Usted _____   Ustedes _____

Frases: _____

_____

_____

_____

_____

_____

_____

_____

_____

_____

_____

Infinitivo _____   ¿Reflejo?   Sí   No

Infinitivo _____ ¿Reflejo?   Sí   No

Significado _____

Pasado participio   Gerundio
(—ado) _____   (—ando) _____

Tiempo verbal _____   ¿Irregular?   Sí   No

Yo _____   Nosotros _____

Tú _____   Vosotros _____

Él, Ella,   Ellos, Ellas,
Usted _____   Ustedes _____

Frases: _____

_____

_____

_____

_____

_____

_____

_____

_____

_____

_____

_____

Infinitivo _____ ¿Reflejo?   Sí   No

Significado _____

Pasado participio   Gerundio
(—ado) _____   (—ando) _____

Tiempo verbal _____ ¿Irregular?   Sí   No

Yo _____   Nosotros _____

Tú _____   Vosotros _____

Él, Ella,   Ellos, Ellas,
Usted _____   Ustedes _____

Frases: _____

_____

_____

_____

_____

_____

_____

_____

_____

_____

_____

Infinitivo _____ ¿Reflejo?   Sí   No

Infinitivo _____   ¿Reflejo?   Sí   No

Significado _____

Pasado participio   Gerundio
(—ado) _____   (—ando) _____

Tiempo verbal _____   ¿Irregular?   Sí   No

Yo _____   Nosotros _____

Tú _____   Vosotros _____

Él, Ella,   Ellos, Ellas,
Usted _____   Ustedes _____

Frases:

_____

_____

_____

_____

_____

_____

_____

_____

_____

_____

Infinitivo _____ ¿Reflejo?   Sí   No

Significado _____

Pasado participio   Gerundio
(—ado)   (—ando)
_____   _____

Tiempo verbal _____   ¿Irregular?   Sí   No

Yo _____   Nosotros _____

Tú _____   Vosotros _____

Él, Ella,   Ellos, Ellas,
Usted _____ Ustedes _____

Frases: _____

_____

_____

_____

_____

_____

_____

_____

_____

_____

_____

_____

Infinitivo _____ ¿Reflejo?   Sí   No

Infinitivo _____ ¿Reflejo?   Sí   No

Significado _____

Pasado participio   Gerundio
(—ado) _____   (—ando) _____

Tiempo verbal _____ ¿Irregular?   Sí   No

Yo _____   Nosotros _____

Tú _____   Vosotros _____

Él, Ella,   Ellos, Ellas,
Usted _____   Ustedes _____

Frases: _____

_____

_____

_____

_____

_____

_____

_____

_____

_____

_____

_____

Infinitivo _____ ¿Reflejo?   Sí   No

Infinitivo _____   ¿Reflejo?   Sí   No

Significado _____

Pasado participio   Gerundio
(—ado) _____   (—ando) _____

Tiempo verbal _____ ¿Irregular?   Sí   No

Yo _____   Nosotros _____

Tú _____   Vosotros _____

Él, Ella,   Ellos, Ellas,
Usted _____   Ustedes _____

Frases:

_____

_____

_____

_____

_____

_____

_____

_____

_____

_____

_____

Infinitivo _____ ¿Reflejo?   Sí   No

Significado _____

Pasado participio _____   Gerundio _____
(—ado)   (—ando)

Tiempo verbal _____ ¿Irregular?   Sí   No

Yo _____   Nosotros _____

Tú _____   Vosotros _____

Él, Ella,   Ellos, Ellas,
Usted _____   Ustedes _____

Frases: _____

_____

_____

_____

_____

_____

_____

_____

_____

_____

_____

_____

_____

Infinitivo _____   ¿Reflejo?   Sí   No

Significado _____

Pasado participio   Gerundio
(—ado) _____   (—ando) _____

Tiempo verbal _____   ¿Irregular?   Sí   No

Yo _____   Nosotros _____

Tú _____   Vosotros _____

Él, Ella,   Ellos, Ellas,
Usted _____   Ustedes _____

Frases: _____

_____

_____

_____

_____

_____

_____

_____

_____

_____

_____

_____

Infinitivo _____ ¿Reflejo?   Sí   No

Significado _____

Pasado participio   Gerundio
(—ado) _____   (—ando) _____

Tiempo verbal _____ ¿Irregular?   Sí   No

Yo _____   Nosotros _____

Tú _____   Vosotros _____

Él, Ella,   Ellos, Ellas,
Usted _____   Ustedes _____

Frases:
_____

_____

_____

_____

_____

_____

_____

_____

_____

_____

_____

_____

Infinitivo _____   ¿Reflejo?   Sí   No

Significado _____

Pasado participio   Gerundio
(—ado) _____   (—ando) _____

Tiempo verbal _____   ¿Irregular?   Sí   No

Yo _____   Nosotros _____

Tú _____   Vosotros _____

Él, Ella,   Ellos, Ellas,
Usted _____   Ustedes _____

Frases: _____

_____

_____

_____

_____

_____

_____

_____

_____

_____

_____

_____

Infinitivo _____ ¿Reflejo? Sí No

Significado _____

Pasado participio _____ Gerundio _____
(—ado)   (—ando)

Tiempo verbal _____ ¿Irregular? Sí No

Yo _____ Nosotros _____

Tú _____ Vosotros _____

Él, Ella, _____ Ellos, Ellas, _____
Usted   Ustedes

Frases: _____

_____

_____

_____

_____

_____

_____

_____

_____

_____

_____

_____

Infinitivo _____   ¿Reflejo?   Sí   No

Significado _____

Pasado participio   Gerundio
(—ado) _____   (—ando) _____

Tiempo verbal _____   ¿Irregular?   Sí   No

Yo _____   Nosotros _____

Tú _____   Vosotros _____

Él, Ella,   Ellos, Ellas,
Usted _____   Ustedes _____

Frases:

_____

_____

_____

_____

_____

_____

_____

_____

_____

_____

_____

Infinitivo _____   ¿Reflejo?   Sí   No

Significado _____

Pasado participio   Gerundio
(—ado) _____   (—ando) _____

Tiempo verbal _____   ¿Irregular?   Sí   No

Yo _____   Nosotros _____

Tú _____   Vosotros _____

Él, Ella,   Ellos, Ellas,
Usted _____   Ustedes _____

Frases:
_____
_____
_____
_____
_____
_____
_____
_____
_____
_____
_____
_____

Infinitivo _____ ¿Reflejo? Sí No

Significado _____

Pasado participio   Gerundio
(—ado) _____   (—ando) _____

Tiempo verbal _____   ¿Irregular? Sí No

Yo _____   Nosotros _____

Tú _____   Vosotros _____

Él, Ella,   Ellos, Ellas,
Usted _____   Ustedes _____

Frases: _____

_____

_____

_____

_____

_____

_____

_____

_____

_____

_____

_____

_____

Infinitivo _____   ¿Reflejo?   Sí   No

Significado _____

Pasado participio   Gerundio
(—ado) _____   (—ando) _____

Tiempo verbal _____   ¿Irregular?   Sí   No

Yo _____   Nosotros _____

Tú _____   Vosotros _____

Él, Ella,   Ellos, Ellas,
Usted _____   Ustedes _____

Frases: _____

_____

_____

_____

_____

_____

_____

_____

_____

_____

_____

_____

Infinitivo _____ ¿Reflejo?   Sí   No

Significado _____

Pasado participio   Gerundio
(—ado) _____   (—ando) _____

Tiempo verbal _____   ¿Irregular?   Sí   No

Yo _____   Nosotros _____

Tú _____   Vosotros _____

Él, Ella,   Ellos, Ellas,
Usted _____   Ustedes _____

Frases: _____

_____

_____

_____

_____

_____

_____

_____

_____

_____

_____

_____

_____

_____

Infinitivo _____   ¿Reflejo?   Sí   No

Significado _____

Pasado participio   Gerundio
(—ado) _____   (—ando) _____

Tiempo verbal _____   ¿Irregular?   Sí   No

Yo _____   Nosotros _____

Tú _____   Vosotros _____

Él, Ella,   Ellos, Ellas,
Usted _____   Ustedes _____

Frases:
_____
_____
_____
_____
_____
_____
_____
_____
_____
_____
_____
_____

Infinitivo _____ ¿Reflejo?   Sí   No

Significado _____

Pasado participio   Gerundio
(—ado) _____   (—ando) _____

Tiempo verbal _____ ¿Irregular?   Sí   No

Yo _____   Nosotros _____

Tú _____   Vosotros _____

Él, Ella,   Ellos, Ellas,
Usted _____   Ustedes _____

Frases: _____

_____

_____

_____

_____

_____

_____

_____

_____

_____

_____

_____

_____

Infinitivo _____   ¿Reflejo?   Sí   No

Significado _____

Pasado participio   Gerundio
(—ado) _____   (—ando) _____

Tiempo verbal _____   ¿Irregular?   Sí   No

Yo _____   Nosotros _____

Tú _____   Vosotros _____

Él, Ella,   Ellos, Ellas,
Usted _____   Ustedes _____

Frases: _____

_____

_____

_____

_____

_____

_____

_____

_____

_____

_____

_____

Infinitivo _____   ¿Reflejo?   Sí   No

Infinitivo _____   ¿Reflejo?   Sí   No

Significado _____

Pasado participio   Gerundio
(—ado) _____   (—ando) _____

Tiempo verbal _____   ¿Irregular?   Sí   No

Yo _____   Nosotros _____

Tú _____   Vosotros _____

Él, Ella,   Ellos, Ellas,
Usted _____   Ustedes _____

Frases: _____

_____

_____

_____

_____

_____

_____

_____

_____

_____

_____

_____

Infinitivo _____

Infinitivo _____ ¿Reflejo?   Sí   No

Significado _____

Pasado participio   Gerundio
(—ado) _____   (—ando) _____

Tiempo verbal _____   ¿Irregular?   Sí   No

Yo _____   Nosotros _____

Tú _____   Vosotros _____

Él, Ella,   Ellos, Ellas,
Usted _____   Ustedes _____

Frases: _____

_____

_____

_____

_____

_____

_____

_____

_____

_____

_____

_____

Infinitivo _____ ¿Reflejo?   Sí   No

Significado _____

Pasado participio   Gerundio
(—ado)   (—ando)
_____   _____

Tiempo verbal _____ ¿Irregular?   Sí   No

Yo _____ Nosotros _____

Tú _____ Vosotros _____

Él, Ella,   Ellos, Ellas,
Usted _____   Ustedes _____

Frases: _____

_____

_____

_____

_____

_____

_____

_____

_____

_____

_____

Infinitivo _____ ¿Reflejo?   Sí   No

Significado _____

Pasado participio   Gerundio
(—ado) _____   (—ando) _____

Tiempo verbal _____ ¿Irregular?   Sí   No

Yo _____   Nosotros _____

Tú _____   Vosotros _____

Él, Ella,   Ellos, Ellas,
Usted _____   Ustedes _____

Frases:

_____

_____

_____

_____

_____

_____

_____

_____

_____

_____

_____

Infinitivo _____ ¿Reflejo?   Sí   No

Infinitivo _____ ¿Reflejo?   Sí   No

Significado _____

Pasado participio   Gerundio
(—ado) _____   (—ando) _____

Tiempo verbal _____   ¿Irregular?   Sí   No

Yo _____   Nosotros _____

Tú _____   Vosotros _____

Él, Ella,   Ellos, Ellas,
Usted _____   Ustedes _____

Frases: _____

_____

_____

_____

_____

_____

_____

_____

_____

_____

_____

_____

_____

Infinitivo _____   ¿Reflejo?   Sí   No

Significado _____

Pasado participio   Gerundio
(—ado) _____   (—ando) _____

Tiempo verbal _____   ¿Irregular?   Sí   No

Yo _____   Nosotros _____

Tú _____   Vosotros _____

Él, Ella,   Ellos, Ellas,
Usted _____   Ustedes _____

Frases: _____

_____

_____

_____

_____

_____

_____

_____

_____

_____

_____

_____

Infinitivo _____   ¿Reflejo?   Sí   No

Significado _____

Pasado participio _____   Gerundio _____
(—ado)   (—ando)

Tiempo verbal _____   ¿Irregular?   Sí   No

Yo _____   Nosotros _____

Tú _____   Vosotros _____

Él, Ella,   Ellos, Ellas,
Usted _____   Ustedes _____

Frases: _____

Infinitivo _____   ¿Reflejo?   Sí   No

Significado _____

Pasado participio   Gerundio
(—ado) _____   (—ando) _____

Tiempo verbal _____   ¿Irregular?   Sí   No

Yo _____   Nosotros _____

Tú _____   Vosotros _____

Él, Ella,   Ellos, Ellas,
Usted _____   Ustedes _____

Frases:
_____
_____
_____
_____
_____
_____
_____
_____
_____
_____
_____
_____

Infinitivo _____   ¿Reflejo?   Sí   No

Significado _____

Pasado participio   Gerundio
(—ado) _____   (—ando) _____

Tiempo verbal _____   ¿Irregular?   Sí   No

Yo _____   Nosotros _____

Tú _____   Vosotros _____

Él, Ella,   Ellos, Ellas,
Usted _____   Ustedes _____

Frases:
_____
_____
_____
_____
_____
_____
_____
_____
_____
_____
_____
_____

Infinitivo _____   ¿Reflejo?   Sí   No

Significado _____

Pasado participio   Gerundio
(—ado) _____   (—ando) _____

Tiempo verbal _____   ¿Irregular?   Sí   No

Yo _____   Nosotros _____

Tú _____   Vosotros _____

Él, Ella,   Ellos, Ellas,
Usted _____   Ustedes _____

Frases: _____

_____

_____

_____

_____

_____

_____

_____

_____

_____

_____

Infinitivo _____   ¿Reflejo?   Sí   No

Significado _____

Pasado participio   Gerundio
(—ado) _____   (—ando) _____

Tiempo verbal _____   ¿Irregular?   Sí   No

Yo _____   Nosotros _____

Tú _____   Vosotros _____

Él, Ella,   Ellos, Ellas,
Usted _____   Ustedes _____

Frases: _____

_____

_____

_____

_____

_____

_____

_____

_____

_____

_____

_____

Infinitivo _____   ¿Reflejo?   Sí   No

Significado _____

Pasado participio _____   Gerundio _____
(—ado)   (—ando)

Tiempo verbal _____   ¿Irregular?   Sí   No

Yo _____   Nosotros _____

Tú _____   Vosotros _____

Él, Ella,   Ellos, Ellas,
Usted _____   Ustedes _____

Frases: _____

_____

_____

_____

_____

_____

_____

_____

_____

_____

_____

Infinitivo _____   ¿Reflejo?   Sí   No

Significado _____

Pasado participio   Gerundio
(—ado) _____   (—ando) _____

Tiempo verbal _____   ¿Irregular?   Sí   No

Yo _____   Nosotros _____

Tú _____   Vosotros _____

Él, Ella,   Ellos, Ellas,
Usted _____   Ustedes _____

Frases: _____

_____

_____

_____

_____

_____

_____

_____

_____

_____

_____

_____

Infinitivo _____ ¿Reflejo?   Sí   No

Significado _____

Pasado participio   Gerundio
(—ado) _____   (—ando) _____

Tiempo verbal _____   ¿Irregular?   Sí   No

Yo _____   Nosotros _____

Tú _____   Vosotros _____

Él, Ella,   Ellos, Ellas,
Usted _____   Ustedes _____

Frases: _____

_____

_____

_____

_____

_____

_____

_____

_____

_____

_____

_____

_____

Infinitivo _____   ¿Reflejo?   Sí   No

Significado _____

Pasado participio   Gerundio
(—ado) _____   (—ando) _____

Tiempo verbal _____   ¿Irregular?   Sí   No

Yo _____   Nosotros _____

Tú _____   Vosotros _____

Él, Ella,   Ellos, Ellas,
Usted _____   Ustedes _____

Frases: _____

_____

_____

_____

_____

_____

_____

_____

_____

_____

_____

Infinitivo _____

Infinitivo _____ ¿Reflejo?   Sí   No

Significado _____

Pasado participio   Gerundio
(—ado) _____   (—ando) _____

Tiempo verbal _____ ¿Irregular?   Sí   No

Yo _____   .   Nosotros _____

Tú _____   Vosotros _____

Él, Ella,   Ellos, Ellas,
Usted _____   Ustedes _____

Frases: _____

_____

_____

_____

_____

_____

_____

_____

_____

_____

_____

_____

Infinitivo _____   ¿Reflejo?   Sí   No

Significado _____

Pasado participio   Gerundio
(—ado) _____   (—ando) _____

Tiempo verbal _____   ¿Irregular?   Sí   No

Yo _____   Nosotros _____

Tú _____   Vosotros _____

Él, Ella,   Ellos, Ellas,
Usted _____   Ustedes _____

Frases: _____

_____

_____

_____

_____

_____

_____

_____

_____

_____

_____

_____

_____

Infinitivo _____   ¿Reflejo?   Sí   No

Significado _____

Infinitivo _____ ¿Reflejo?   Sí   No

Significado _____

Pasado participio   Gerundio
(—ado) _____   (—ando) _____

Tiempo verbal _____ ¿Irregular?   Sí   No

Yo _____   Nosotros _____

Tú _____   Vosotros _____

Él, Ella,   Ellos, Ellas,
Usted _____   Ustedes _____

Frases:
_____

_____

_____

_____

_____

_____

_____

_____

_____

_____

_____

_____

Infinitivo _____ ¿Reflejo? Sí No

Significado _____

Pasado participio   Gerundio
(—ado) _____   (—ando) _____

Tiempo verbal _____   ¿Irregular? Sí No

Yo _____   Nosotros _____

Tú _____   Vosotros _____

Él, Ella,   Ellos, Ellas,
Usted _____   Ustedes _____

Frases: _____

_____

_____

_____

_____

_____

_____

_____

_____

_____

_____

_____

_____

Infinitivo _____ ¿Reflejo?   Sí   No

Significado _____

Pasado participio _____ Gerundio _____
(—ado)   (—ando)

Tiempo verbal _____ ¿Irregular?   Sí   No

Yo _____ Nosotros _____

Tú _____ Vosotros _____

Él, Ella, _____ Ellos, Ellas, _____
Usted   Ustedes

Frases: _____

_____

_____

_____

_____

_____

_____

_____

_____

_____

_____

_____

Infinitivo _____   ¿Reflejo?   Sí   No

Significado _____

Pasado participio   Gerundio
(—ado) _____   (—ando) _____

Tiempo verbal _____   ¿Irregular?   Sí   No

Yo _____   Nosotros _____

Tú _____   Vosotros _____

Él, Ella,   Ellos, Ellas,
Usted _____   Ustedes _____

Frases: _____

_____

_____

_____

_____

_____

_____

_____

_____

_____

_____

_____

Infinitivo _____ ¿Reflejo?   Sí   No

Significado _____

Pasado participio   Gerundio
(—ado) _____   (—ando) _____

Tiempo verbal _____ ¿Irregular?   Sí   No

Yo _____   Nosotros _____

Tú _____   Vosotros _____

Él, Ella,   Ellos, Ellas,
Usted _____   Ustedes _____

Frases:
_____

_____

_____

_____

_____

_____

_____

_____

_____

_____

_____

_____

Infinitivo _____ ¿Reflejo?   Sí   No

Significado _____

Pasado participio   Gerundio
(—ado) _____   (—ando) _____

Tiempo verbal _____ ¿Irregular?   Sí   No

Yo _____   Nosotros _____

Tú _____   Vosotros _____

Él, Ella,   Ellos, Ellas,
Usted _____   Ustedes _____

Frases:

_____

_____

_____

_____

_____

_____

_____

_____

_____

_____

_____

_____

Infinitivo _____ ¿Reflejo?   Sí   No

Significado _____

Pasado participio _____ Gerundio _____
(—ado)   (—ando)

Tiempo verbal _____ ¿Irregular?   Sí   No

Yo _____ Nosotros _____

Tú _____ Vosotros _____

Él, Ella,   Ellos, Ellas,
Usted _____   Ustedes _____

Frases: _____

_____

_____

_____

_____

_____

_____

_____

_____

_____

_____

_____

Infinitivo _____ ¿Reflejo? Sí No

Significado _____

Pasado participio   Gerundio
(—ado) _____   (—ando) _____

Tiempo verbal _____   ¿Irregular? Sí No

Yo _____   Nosotros _____

Tú _____   Vosotros _____

Él, Ella,   Ellos, Ellas,
Usted _____   Ustedes _____

Frases: _____

_____

_____

_____

_____

_____

_____

_____

_____

_____

_____

Infinitivo _____   ¿Reflejo?   Sí   No

Significado _____

Pasado participio _____   Gerundio _____
(—ado)   (—ando)

Tiempo verbal _____   ¿Irregular?   Sí   No

Yo _____   Nosotros _____

Tú _____   Vosotros _____

Él, Ella,   _____   Ellos, Ellas,   _____
Usted   Ustedes

Frases: _____

_____

_____

_____

_____

_____

_____

_____

_____

_____

_____

_____

Infinitivo _____ ¿Reflejo?   Sí   No

Significado _____

Pasado participio   Gerundio
(—ado) _____   (—ando) _____

Tiempo verbal _____   ¿Irregular?   Sí   No

Yo _____   Nosotros _____

Tú _____   Vosotros _____

Él, Ella,   Ellos, Ellas,
Usted _____   Ustedes _____

Frases: _____

_____

_____

_____

_____

_____

_____

_____

_____

_____

_____

_____

_____

_____

Infinitivo _____ ¿Reflejo?   Sí   No

Infinitivo _____   ¿Reflejo?   Sí   No

Significado _____

Pasado participio   Gerundio
(—ado) _____   (—ando) _____

Tiempo verbal _____   ¿Irregular?   Sí   No

Yo _____   Nosotros _____

Tú _____   Vosotros _____

Él, Ella,   Ellos, Ellas,
Usted _____   Ustedes _____

Frases:
_____

_____

_____

_____

_____

_____

_____

_____

_____

_____

_____

Infinitivo _____ ¿Reflejo? Sí No

Significado _____

Pasado participio   Gerundio
(—ado) _____   (—ando) _____

Tiempo verbal _____ ¿Irregular? Sí No

Yo _____   Nosotros _____

Tú _____   Vosotros _____

Él, Ella,   Ellos, Ellas,
Usted _____   Ustedes _____

Frases: _____

_____

_____

_____

_____

_____

_____

_____

_____

_____

_____

_____

_____

Infinitivo _____ ¿Reflejo?   Sí   No

Significado _____

Pasado participio   Gerundio
(—ado) _____   (—ando) _____

Tiempo verbal _____   ¿Irregular?   Sí   No

Yo _____   Nosotros _____

Tú _____   Vosotros _____

Él, Ella,   Ellos, Ellas,
Usted _____   Ustedes _____

Frases: _____

_____

_____

_____

_____

_____

_____

_____

_____

_____

_____

Infinitivo _____ ¿Reflejo? Sí No

Significado _____

Pasado participio   Gerundio
(—ado) _____ (—ando) _____

Tiempo verbal _____ ¿Irregular? Sí No

Yo _____ Nosotros _____

Tú _____ Vosotros _____

Él, Ella,   Ellos, Ellas,
Usted _____ Ustedes _____

Frases: _____

_____

_____

_____

_____

_____

_____

_____

_____

_____

_____

_____

_____

_____

Infinitivo _____ ¿Reflejo?   Sí   No

Significado _____

Pasado participio   Gerundio
(—ado) _____   (—ando) _____

Tiempo verbal _____   ¿Irregular?   Sí   No

Yo _____   Nosotros _____

Tú _____   Vosotros _____

Él, Ella,   Ellos, Ellas,
Usted _____   Ustedes _____

Frases: _____

_____

_____

_____

_____

_____

_____

_____

_____

_____

_____

_____

_____

Infinitivo _____   ¿Reflejo?   Sí   No

Significado _____

Pasado participio   Gerundio
(—ado) _____   (—ando) _____

Tiempo verbal _____   ¿Irregular?   Sí   No

Yo _____   Nosotros _____

Tú _____   Vosotros _____

Él, Ella,   Ellos, Ellas,
Usted _____   Ustedes _____

Frases:

_____

_____

_____

_____

_____

_____

_____

_____

_____

_____

_____

_____

Infinitivo _____   ¿Reflejo?   Sí   No

Infinitivo _____ ¿Reflejo?   Sí   No

Significado _____

Pasado participio   Gerundio
(—ado)   (—ando)
_____   _____

Tiempo verbal _____ ¿Irregular?   Sí   No

Yo _____   Nosotros _____

Tú _____   Vosotros _____

Él, Ella,   Ellos, Ellas,
Usted _____ Ustedes _____

Frases: _____

_____

_____

_____

_____

_____

_____

_____

_____

_____

_____

_____

_____

Infinitivo _____   ¿Reflejo?   Sí   No

Significado _____

Pasado participio   Gerundio
(—ado) _____   (—ando) _____

Tiempo verbal _____   ¿Irregular?   Sí   No

Yo _____   Nosotros _____

Tú _____   Vosotros _____

Él, Ella,   Ellos, Ellas,
Usted _____   Ustedes _____

Frases:
_____
_____
_____
_____
_____
_____
_____
_____
_____
_____
_____

Infinitivo _____   ¿Reflejo?   Sí   No

Infinitivo _____   ¿Reflejo?   Sí   No

Significado _____

Pasado participio   Gerundio
(—ado) _____   (—ando) _____

Tiempo verbal _____   ¿Irregular?   Sí   No

Yo _____   Nosotros _____

Tú _____   Vosotros _____

Él, Ella,   Ellos, Ellas,
Usted _____   Ustedes _____

Frases:

_____

_____

_____

_____

_____

_____

_____

_____

_____

_____

_____

_____

Infinitivo _____   ¿Reflejo?   Sí   No

Significado _____

Pasado participio   Gerundio
(—ado) _____   (—ando) _____

Tiempo verbal _____   ¿Irregular?   Sí   No

Yo _____   Nosotros _____

Tú _____   Vosotros _____

Él, Ella,   Ellos, Ellas,
Usted _____   Ustedes _____

Frases: _____

_____

_____

_____

_____

_____

_____

_____

_____

_____

_____

_____

_____

Infinitivo _____ ¿Reflejo?   Sí   No

Significado _____

Pasado participio _____ Gerundio _____
(—ado)   (—ando)

Tiempo verbal _____ ¿Irregular?   Sí   No

Yo _____ Nosotros _____

Tú _____ Vosotros _____

Él, Ella, _____ Ellos, Ellas, _____
Usted   Ustedes

Frases: _____

_____

_____

_____

_____

_____

_____

_____

_____

_____

_____

_____

Infinitivo _____ ¿Reflejo?   Sí   No

Significado _____

Pasado participio   Gerundio
(—ado) _____   (—ando) _____

Tiempo verbal _____   ¿Irregular?   Sí   No

Yo _____   Nosotros _____

Tú _____   Vosotros _____

Él, Ella,   Ellos, Ellas,
Usted _____   Ustedes _____

Frases:
_____
_____
_____
_____
_____
_____
_____
_____
_____
_____
_____
_____

Infinitivo _____   ¿Reflejo?   Sí   No

Significado _____

Pasado participio   Gerundio
(—ado) _____   (—ando) _____

Tiempo verbal _____   ¿Irregular?   Sí   No

Yo _____   Nosotros _____

Tú _____   Vosotros _____

Él, Ella,   Ellos, Ellas,
Usted _____   Ustedes _____

Frases:

_____

_____

_____

_____

_____

_____

_____

_____

_____

_____

_____

_____

Infinitivo _____   ¿Reflejo?   Sí   No

Significado _____

Pasado participio   Gerundio
(—ado) _____   (—ando) _____

Tiempo verbal _____   ¿Irregular?   Sí   No

Yo _____   Nosotros _____

Tú _____   Vosotros _____

Él, Ella,   Ellos, Ellas,
Usted _____   Ustedes _____

Frases: _____

_____

_____

_____

_____

_____

_____

_____

_____

_____

_____

_____

Infinitivo _____   ¿Reflejo?   Sí   No

Infinitivo _____   ¿Reflejo?   Sí   No

Significado _____

Pasado participio   Gerundio
(—ado) _____   (—ando) _____

Tiempo verbal _____   ¿Irregular?   Sí   No

Yo _____   Nosotros _____

Tú _____   Vosotros _____

Él, Ella,   Ellos, Ellas,
Usted _____   Ustedes _____

Frases:
_____
_____
_____
_____
_____
_____
_____
_____
_____
_____
_____
_____

Infinitivo _____ ¿Reflejo?   Sí   No

Significado _____

Pasado participio   Gerundio
(—ado) _____   (—ando) _____

Tiempo verbal _____ ¿Irregular?   Sí   No

Yo _____   Nosotros _____

Tú _____   Vosotros _____

Él, Ella,   Ellos, Ellas,
Usted _____   Ustedes _____

Frases: _____

_____

_____

_____

_____

_____

_____

_____

_____

_____

_____

Infinitivo _____   ¿Reflejo?   Sí   No

Significado _____

Pasado participio   Gerundio
(—ado) _____   (—ando) _____

Tiempo verbal _____   ¿Irregular?   Sí   No

Yo _____   Nosotros _____

Tú _____   Vosotros _____

Él, Ella,   Ellos, Ellas,
Usted _____   Ustedes _____

Frases:
_____

_____

_____

_____

_____

_____

_____

_____

_____

_____

_____

_____

_____

Infinitivo _____   ¿Reflejo?   Sí   No

Significado _____

Pasado participio   Gerundio
(—ado) _____   (—ando) _____

Tiempo verbal _____   ¿Irregular?   Sí   No

Yo _____   Nosotros _____

Tú _____   Vosotros _____

Él, Ella,   Ellos, Ellas,
Usted _____   Ustedes _____

Frases: _____

_____

_____

_____

_____

_____

_____

_____

_____

_____

_____

_____

_____

_____   ¿Reflejo?   Sí   No

Significado _____

Infinitivo _____   ¿Reflejo?   Sí   No

Significado _____

Pasado participio   Gerundio
(—ado) _____   (—ando) _____

Tiempo verbal _____   ¿Irregular?   Sí   No

Yo _____   Nosotros _____

Tú _____   Vosotros _____

Él, Ella,   Ellos, Ellas,
Usted _____   Ustedes _____

Frases: _____

_____

_____

_____

_____

_____

_____

_____

_____

_____

_____

_____

Infinitivo _____   ¿Reflejo?   Sí   No

Significado _____

Pasado participio   Gerundio
(—ado) _____   (—ando) _____

Tiempo verbal _____   ¿Irregular?   Sí   No

Yo _____   Nosotros _____

Tú _____   Vosotros _____

Él, Ella,   Ellos, Ellas,
Usted _____   Ustedes _____

Frases: _____

_____

_____

_____

_____

_____

_____

_____

_____

_____

_____

_____

Infinitivo _____ ¿Reflejo?   Sí   No

Significado _____

Pasado participio   Gerundio
(—ado) _____   (—ando) _____

Tiempo verbal _____   ¿Irregular?   Sí   No

Yo _____   Nosotros _____

Tú _____   Vosotros _____

Él, Ella,   Ellos, Ellas,
Usted _____   Ustedes _____

Frases: _____

_____

_____

_____

_____

_____

_____

_____

_____

_____

_____

_____

_____

_____

Infinitivo _____ ¿Reflejo?   Sí   No

Significado _____

Pasado participio   Gerundio
(—ado) _____   (—ando) _____

Tiempo verbal _____   ¿Irregular?   Sí   No

Yo _____   Nosotros _____

Tú _____   Vosotros _____

Él, Ella,   Ellos, Ellas,
Usted _____   Ustedes _____

Frases: _____

_____

_____

_____

_____

_____

_____

_____

_____

_____

_____

_____

_____

_____

Infinitivo _____   ¿Reflejo?   Sí   No

Significado _____

Pasado participio   Gerundio
(—ado) _____   (—ando) _____

Tiempo verbal _____   ¿Irregular?   Sí   No

Yo _____   Nosotros _____

Tú _____   Vosotros _____

Él, Ella,   Ellos, Ellas,
Usted _____   Ustedes _____

Frases: _____

_____

_____

_____

_____

_____

_____

_____

_____

_____

_____

_____

_____

Infinitivo _____ ¿Reflejo?   Sí   No

Significado _____

Pasado participio _____   Gerundio _____
(—ado)   (—ando)

Tiempo verbal _____   ¿Irregular?   Sí   No

Yo _____   Nosotros _____

Tú _____   Vosotros

Él, Ella,   Ellos, Ellas,
Usted _____   Ustedes _____

Frases:

_____

_____

_____

_____

_____

_____

_____

_____

_____

_____

_____

_____

Infinitivo _____ ¿Reflejo?   Sí   No

Significado _____

Infinitivo _____   ¿Reflejo?   Sí   No

Significado _____

Pasado participio   Gerundio
(—ado) _____   (—ando) _____

Tiempo verbal _____   ¿Irregular?   Sí   No

Yo _____   Nosotros _____

Tú _____   Vosotros _____

Él, Ella,   Ellos, Ellas,
Usted _____   Ustedes _____

Frases: _____

_____

_____

_____

_____

_____

_____

_____

_____

_____

_____

_____

Infinitivo _____ ¿Reflejo?   Sí   No

Significado _____

Pasado participio   Gerundio
(—ado) _____   (—ando) _____

Tiempo verbal _____ ¿Irregular?   Sí   No

Yo _____   Nosotros _____

Tú _____   Vosotros _____

Él, Ella,   Ellos, Ellas,
Usted _____   Ustedes _____

Frases: _____

_____

_____

_____

_____

_____

_____

_____

_____

_____

_____

_____

_____

Infinitivo _____ ¿Reflejo?   Sí   No

Significado _____

Pasado participio   Gerundio
(—ado) _____   (—ando) _____

Tiempo verbal _____ ¿Irregular?   Sí   No

Yo _____   Nosotros _____

Tú _____   Vosotros _____

Él, Ella,   Ellos, Ellas,
Usted _____   Ustedes _____

Frases:
_____
_____
_____
_____
_____
_____
_____
_____
_____
_____
_____
_____

Infinitivo _____ ¿Reflejo?   Sí   No

Infinitivo _____   ¿Reflejo?   Sí   No

Significado _____

Pasado participio   Gerundio
(—ado) _____   (—ando) _____

Tiempo verbal _____   ¿Irregular?   Sí   No

Yo _____   Nosotros _____

Tú _____   Vosotros _____

Él, Ella,   Ellos, Ellas,
Usted _____   Ustedes _____

Frases: _____

_____

_____

_____

_____

_____

_____

_____

_____

_____

_____

_____

_____

Infinitivo _____   ¿Reflejo?   Sí   No

Infinitivo _____ ¿Reflejo? Sí No

Significado _____

Pasado participio   Gerundio
(—ado) _____   (—ando) _____

Tiempo verbal _____   ¿Irregular? Sí No

Yo _____   Nosotros _____

Tú _____   Vosotros _____

Él, Ella,   Ellos, Ellas,
Usted _____   Ustedes _____

Frases:

_____

_____

_____

_____

_____

_____

_____

_____

_____

_____

_____

Infinitivo _____ ¿Reflejo?   Sí   No

Significado _____

Pasado participio   Gerundio
(—ado) _____   (—ando) _____

Tiempo verbal _____ ¿Irregular?   Sí   No

Yo _____   Nosotros _____

Tú _____   Vosotros _____

Él, Ella,   Ellos, Ellas,
Usted _____   Ustedes _____

Frases: _____

_____

_____

_____

_____

_____

_____

_____

_____

_____

_____

_____

_____

Infinitivo _____   ¿Reflejo?   Sí   No

Significado _____

Pasado participio   Gerundio
(—ado) _____   (—ando) _____

Tiempo verbal _____   ¿Irregular?   Sí   No

Yo _____   Nosotros _____

Tú _____   Vosotros _____

Él, Ella,   Ellos, Ellas,
Usted _____   Ustedes _____

Frases: _____

_____

_____

_____

_____

_____

_____

_____

_____

_____

_____

_____

Infinitivo _____ ¿Reflejo?   Sí   No

Significado _____

Pasado participio   Gerundio
(—ado) _____   (—ando) _____

Tiempo verbal _____   ¿Irregular?   Sí   No

Yo _____	Nosotros _____	
Tú _____	Vosotros _____	
Él, Ella, Usted _____	Ellos, Ellas, Ustedes _____	

Frases:

_____

_____

_____

_____

_____

_____

_____

_____

_____

_____

_____

_____

_____

_____

Infinitivo _____ ¿Reflejo?   Sí   No

Significado _____

Pasado participio   Gerundio
(—ado) _____   (—ando) _____

Tiempo verbal _____   ¿Irregular?   Sí   No

Yo _____   Nosotros _____

Tú _____   Vosotros _____

Él, Ella,   Ellos, Ellas,
Usted _____   Ustedes _____

Frases: _____

_____

_____

_____

_____

_____

_____

_____

_____

_____

_____

Infinitivo _____ ¿Reflejo?   Sí   No

Infinitivo _____ ¿Reflejo?   Sí   No

Significado _____

Pasado participio   Gerundio
(—ado) _____   (—ando) _____

Tiempo verbal _____ ¿Irregular?   Sí   No

Yo _____   Nosotros _____

Tú _____   Vosotros _____

Él, Ella,   Ellos, Ellas,
Usted _____   Ustedes _____

Frases: _____

_____

_____

_____

_____

_____

_____

_____

_____

_____

_____

Infinitivo _____ ¿Reflejo?   Sí   No

Significado

Infinitivo _____   ¿Reflejo?   Sí   No

Significado _____

Pasado participio   Gerundio
(—ado) _____   (—ando) _____

Tiempo verbal _____   ¿Irregular?   Sí   No

Yo _____   Nosotros _____

Tú _____   Vosotros _____

Él, Ella,   Ellos, Ellas,
Usted _____   Ustedes _____

Frases:

_____

_____

_____

_____

_____

_____

_____

_____

_____

_____

_____

Infinitivo _____ ¿Reflejo?   Sí   No

Significado _____

Pasado participio   Gerundio
(—ado) _____   (—ando) _____

Tiempo verbal _____ ¿Irregular?   Sí   No

Yo _____   Nosotros _____

Tú _____   Vosotros _____

Él, Ella,   Ellos, Ellas,
Usted _____   Ustedes _____

Frases:
_____

_____

_____

_____

_____

_____

_____

_____

_____

_____

_____

Infinitivo _____   ¿Reflejo?   Sí   No

Significado _____

Pasado participio   Gerundio
(—ado) _____   (—ando) _____

Tiempo verbal _____   ¿Irregular?   Sí   No

Yo _____   Nosotros _____

Tú _____   Vosotros _____

Él, Ella,   Ellos, Ellas,
Usted _____   Ustedes _____

Frases:

_____

_____

_____

_____

_____

_____

_____

_____

_____

_____

_____

21 countries have Spanish as their official language.
From the largest in area to the smallest they are

México	República Dominicana
Colombia	Honduras
España	Paraguay
Argentina	El Salvador
Perú	Nicaragua
Venezuela	Costa Rica
Chile	Panamá
Ecuador	Uruguay
Guatemala	Puerto Rico
Cuba	Guinea Ecuatorial
Bolivia	

Spanish is also frequently used in
the United States of America and in Belize.

I hope you have taught yourself a lot.
Happy journeying through the fascinating Spanish-speaking world!

Susan Stubb

Made in the USA
Middletown, DE
09 December 2023

45089096R00068